CONNECTIONS

a child's natural learning tool

JANE BASKWILL

SCHOLASTIC

Toronto • Sydney • New York • London • Auckland

To Paulette
who often acts as a sounding board for my connections

Scholastic-TAB Publications Ltd.
123 Newkirk Road, Richmond Hill, Ontario, Canada L4C 3G5

Scholastic Inc.
730 Broadway, New York, NY 10003, USA

Ashton Scholastic Limited
Private Bag 1, Penrose, Auckland 6, New Zealand

Ashton Scholastic Pty Limited
PO Box 579, Gosford, NSW, 2250, Australia

Scholastic Publications Ltd.
Holly Walk, Leamington Spa, Warwickshire CV32 4LS, England

This book is based on a series of articles published in *Teaching Pre K-8*

Cover by Dorothy Siemens

Canadian Cataloguing in Publication Data

Baskwill, Jane
    Connections: a child's natural learning tool

(New directions)
ISBN 0-590-73458-X

1. Learning. 2. Interdisciplinary approach in education.
I. Title. II. Series: New directions (Richmond Hill, Ont.).

LB1060.B38 1990   370.15'23   C90-093820-X

Contents

Children connect

Sarah, Joel, Kyla and Jodi are at the sand table.
"Let's make a tunnel," Joel suggests.
Sarah begins piling sand in the center of the table.
"We'll need to wet it," Jodi states knowingly, "so it will stick together."
"I made a sand tunnel at the beach," Kyla adds, "but I didn't wet the sand enough. When I got to the middle the whole thing collapsed — the sand inside was still dry."
"Like the newspaper on the painting table yesterday," Sarah contributes. "When I threw the paper away the bottom one was still dry!"
"Maybe we should mix the water and the sand before we pile it, to be sure it's all wet."
"Like making a cake," Jodi offers. "When you pour the wet stuff on the flour it sort of sits there until you mix it. Maybe if we mix the sand and water it'll all get wet."
"And if it doesn't, we'll know we need more water . . ."

Children are always making connections. They connect what happened yesterday with what's happening today; they connect their own experience with someone else's; they apply what they know about one situation to many others; they predict what might happen in a new situation and then adjust their predictions and explanations in the light of new observations.

In the above vignette, these five-year-olds demonstrate their knowledge of the basic properties of sand and how it interacts with water. They pool their knowledge, extend each others' experience and solve the problem at hand. They are making connections between what they know and the task at hand.

1

An interrelated curriculum

In the classroom, one way to capitalize on the natural ability of children to make both broad and specific connections is to develop an "interrelated curriculum" that can pull the content areas together through the use of themes, with the language arts strand providing the glue that binds the whole program together.

Much has been written recently about the integration of subject matter — the breaking down of lines separating science, social studies, mathematics and language arts — and many whole language teachers have moved in that direction. But some people are concerned that the end result will be a watering down of the disciplines, and of content.

I don't agree. My experience has shown that an interrelated curriculum allows and encourages the development of natural relationships among subjects, and these connections broaden the theme as new avenues are explored. An interrelated approach naturally includes required curricula in a meaningful, not isolated way. In fact, ties between the disciplines are strengthened rather than diluted. When a particular focus is part of a much broader one, children can more readily see connections, relationships and implications. They respond more readily to opportunities to explore the languages of science, social studies and math, and develop strategies for understanding and coping with those materials.

What *is* necessary, however, is that we provide a rich environment with lots of hands-on experiences, many opportunities to question and discuss, and a variety of legitimate texts — fiction, non-fiction, expository, narrative. And that environment needs to be carefully planned to ensure ample materials for anticipated areas of interest.

Planning

I follow a definite procedure when I plan a theme:

- First I brainstorm, usually with the help of a colleague, since a lot more ideas come up that way. During the brainstorming I try not to think of the classroom. This may sound a little odd, but I find I think of a lot more possibilities when I'm not trying to make my thinking conform to the school curriculum. There'll be plenty of time for that later.

- Next I determine the theme's principal focus areas: where it might begin, what might come next, where it might end. I try to organize the theme so it moves logically and naturally from one area of study to another. During a "Sea" theme, for example, we might look at the properties of water in the ocean, at life above and on the ocean, at life beneath it, at recreation associated with it. Focusing on specific areas means I'm not jumping from one idea or concept to the next and then retracing my steps a few days later. By having a general idea where the theme is going, I'm able to anticipate needs that may arise and have lots of materials on hand.

- Then I list possible literature — the poems, songs and stories that we might use during shared language sessions. At this time I also take stock of any professional resources I may have on hand or be able to borrow.

- Finally I lay out a 20-day plan for the language arts segment of the theme.

I call this whole process "themestorming." (For more on my concept of themestorming see the August/September 1988 issue of *Teaching Pre K-8*.) I've used a thematic approach for more than eight years now, but I still systematically go through themestorming for every new theme I consider. Even when I re-evaluate or modify a theme I've already used, I go through the same procedure.

Beyond language arts

In the beginning, when I was first getting myself organized, my planning didn't go beyond the language arts part of my program. Elements from other curriculum areas appeared purely by accident and usually turned out to be more language arts than genuine science, social studies or math. But over the last few years I've made deliberate efforts — whenever it seemed appropriate — to include other disciplines. I look for materials and literature that encourage consideration of the theme from the point of view of a scientist, social scientist or mathematician. I'm no longer satisfied with superficial references to a particular concept, and I deliberately plan for opportunities to see how a concept specific to one discipline might relate to a situation or concept specific to another. This approach has helped me get away from dependance on text books as the basis of my science, social studies and math programs. I now look at concepts and strategies rather than at chapter numbers.

Some whole language teachers suggest that divisions within the school day for science, math and social studies are purely artificial and don't reflect the real world outside the classroom, and there may be great merit in that argument. However, as both a school administrator and a teacher, I must be concerned with the guidelines determined by my provincial Department of Education, and ensure that I don't inadvertently neglect a particular curriculum area. Let's face it, many teachers dislike particular areas of the curriculum — perhaps because they feel intimidated. Science is a prime example. Some teachers choose to avoid science whenever possible. But I schedule a definite time for it, to be certain I'm doing justice to it.

After my initial themestorming, planning for other curriculum areas becomes relatively simple:

- I look more closely at my themestorming and determine which focus areas lend themselves to further exploration during time designated for other disciplines. At that point I look at my provincial curriculum guides and select concepts that relate.
- Then I brainstorm routines and long-term activities that might be appropriate for each curriculum area. Particular themes may lean more in the direction of one discipline than another — science, for example, rather than social studies. I keep that in mind as I select themes over the course of the year so that one curriculum area doesn't outbalance the others.
- Next I follow my usual language arts procedure and brainstorm the literature. Since I've found that non-fiction texts don't come to mind as readily as storybooks, most often I have to ask the local librarian for help to find additional pieces. Taking one curriculum area at a time, I select particular pieces of literature I feel will be useful.
- Finally I decide what routines I might use with each piece of literature.

You might recognize the word "routine" from its initial use in the *Whole Language Sourcebook,* defined there as *succinct, specific, smooth bits of instruction.* Other writers have used terms like "mini-demonstrations" or "mini-lessons" for very similar activities.

The routines described in the *Sourcebook* are almost exclusively language arts routines, intended to provide children with opportunities to explore print as readers and writers. Through those explorations children develop strategies for dealing with print on their own, or for generating similar texts. Most of them are based on fictional material.

I recently began to realize that these routines can be extended for use in the curriculum areas as well, that they are useful ways for developing in children a confidence that they can read and write as scientists, social scientists or mathematicians. So now I depend on those routines, and additional ones, for helping children to learn the language of whatever discipline we're involved with, and to develop competence in thinking in that language. As a Micmac expression has it, "You think the language you speak." And I want my children to be comfortable thinking and speaking in a variety of languages.

Once I've settled on routines, my themestorming is complete: I have a plan that encompasses not only language arts, but math, science and social studies as well. I also have at my fingertips a variety of resource materials, trade books and activities to spark further exploration. Now that I've planned, I can be comfortable with the natural spontaneity of the children and allow the theme to grow naturally in pace with their needs and interests.

Now that my language arts themes are interrelated with the other curriculum areas, I find that they contain enough resources to extend over a longer period of time. An interrelated theme usually lasts for about two months. I usually plan for five different themes over the course of the school year.

I've learned a great deal about theme selection since I started extending them as well. I find the title of a theme is especially important, since it triggers the whole themestorming process. A theme title such as "Mysteries," for example, gets me thinking about whodunits, Sherlock Holmes and detectives in general. If that title changes to "It's a Mystery," I'm encouraged to think more widely: about how caterpillars change into butterflies, about Stonehenge, the Bermuda Triangle, the pyramids, and other mysteries of science and civilization. The title frees my imagination and sets in motion a series of connections beyond a genre or specific topic.

So now my theme titles sound more like book or song titles: "Sally Go Round the Sun," "Down in the Valley," "Take Flight," "Country Roads," rather than topic headings: "Space," "Apples," "Travel," etc.

Because each theme has such a broad base, I can now see interrelationships between themes as well as between curriculum areas and create a more cohesive program over the course of the year.

The curriculum becomes more of a spiral: as topics and concepts reappear we explore them from new vantage points. For instance, "Weather," a favorite theme at the lower elementary grades, is no longer a theme on its own but, more appropriately, a topic that comes back time and again, relating to farming, navigation and fishing, the demise of the dinosaurs, flight and the launching of weather satellites, etc. "Weather" becomes more than the change of seasons; it becomes an important part of the life and livelihood of living things. Each time children explore a topic they add to the knowledge they already have of it, and can see the relationships inherent in their explorations.

Organizing themes for an interrelated curriculum draws on the inherent ability children have to see the connectedness within their world, and thus helps them make sense of it.

Routines

My collection of resources for any theme becomes, first and foremost, an easily accessible general classroom resource. But I use the books for specific purposes as well, with specific routines. I've found two types of routines particularly useful in the curriculum areas: "launchers" and "mini-demonstrations."

Launchers

A good theme launcher will help you get into a theme, steer it in a new direction, or focus on a particular aspect of it. There are many excellent non-fiction trade books that lend themselves well to launcher routines, to fill a variety of purposes. For example, they can:

- demonstrate a concept;
- pose a question that begs to be answered;
- suggest a relationship to something else within the children's experience.

As with the poems, songs and stories I use during shared language sessions, I gather the children around me in the book area so they can be as close as possible to the text. Whenever I can I use an overhead or opaque projector so the children can see both the print and the illustrations.

Ruth Heller's books are especially good launchers. Several, for instance, deal with various aspects of sea life: mammals of the sea *(Animals Born Alive and Well)*, underwater egg-layers *(Chickens Aren't the Only Ones)*, seaweed *(Plants That Never Ever Bloom)*, underwater camouflage *(How to Hide an Octopus)*. Using these books at various times during the theme, with specific routines, allows the children not only to explore those aspects of sea life, but also to make connections between them, and between them and other natural occurences. At the same time they make natural connections to their previous knowledge and experiences.

Brainstorming

Brainstorming is the rapid and spontaneous generation of ideas. It has long been used by scientists in "think tanks" to generate new projects or alternative solutions to problems. Brainstormed ideas usually range from the obvious to the sublime. That's what makes the technique so effective, since out of something remote may come an outstanding idea.

Brainstorming is often used as a pre-writing or pre-reading tool in language arts, where it helps learners take stock of what they already know. By adding semantic webbing or some other form of organization to the results of brainstorming, we can also demonstrate to children how to organize their thinking.

To help children become comfortable brainstormers in science, social studies or math, I may first use a launcher that demonstrates the use of brainstorming; the Ruth Heller books provide excellent examples of that as well. *The Icky Bug Book, The Bird Alphabet Book* and *The Ocean Alphabet Book* by Jerry Palotta also present an organized brainstorming format.

Such books set brainstorming in motion, prime the pump and create a desire to continue the process for a particular topic or theme. They may even create a desire to begin brainstorming for a different topic or an offshoot of the one found in the book the children are dealing with. For example, since dinosaurs were animals that laid eggs, following the reading of *Chickens Aren't the Only Ones* the children easily launch into brainstorming of the topic "extinct egg-layers."

Charts and graphs

Charts and graphs are usually thought to fall within the domain of science and social studies, since they provide a simple way of visually presenting information gathered or observed.

A launcher that demonstrates the use of this tool in a non-fiction context is *Growing Radishes and Carrots* by Faye Bolton and Diane Snowball. This book not only shows, in both text and illustrations, how one goes about planting and caring for these vegetables, it also uses a time chart to present information about the rate of growth from seeds to vegetables.

We decided to use a similar chart in our book about dinosaurs to show a comparison of the sizes of various dinosaurs. By looking at several different kinds of charts, on a variety of topics, and analyzing the information each one presented, we were able to decide how we wanted to present our own information.

Interpretation

An understanding of science and social studies (or any other discipline for that matter) need not be confined to obvious factual information and non-fiction reading material. An appreciation for nature and the variety of life forms on this planet, as well as for the amazing way the world and its species fit together, can also be enhanced through responding to that information in the form of music, movement, art, etc. *What the Sea Left Behind* (Mimi Gregoire Carpenter) allows us to enjoy the life found on a seashore through a mother and child who collect items from the beach and use them in artistic presentations. *Notes from a Field Naturalist's Sketchbook* (Clare Walker Leslie) and *The Seaside Naturalist* (Deborah Coulombe) relate art to the observation of living things and geographical formations. Both of these make effective launchers.

Common Ground, a recording by Paul Winter, blends the sounds of animals in the wild with the sounds of musical accompaniment to give a feeling for those wild creatures. Using it to accompany movement and painting will result in an interpretative appreciation for nature in its many forms.

Labeling

During language arts, the labeling routine serves to draw attention to descriptive terms as the children develop words or phrases to describe particular parts of a drawing, as in this design for a spaghetti machine:

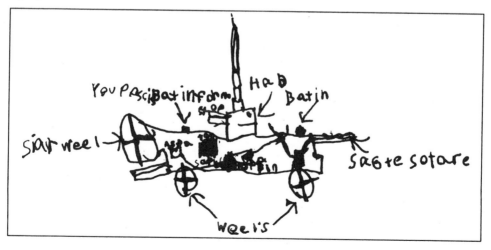

In science, social studies and math, labeling becomes a tool for including specific information that may be necessary for fuller understanding of a diagram or drawing.

There are many examples of labeling in non-fiction texts. I've used Olivier Dunrae's *Skara Brae,* for example, in a "Homes" theme. During a social studies period the book became a means of looking at how someone describing the dwellings in that settlement labeled his drawings for clarity. We speculated that the reason the author/illustrator did this was that homes of that period would be unfamiliar to us and the labeling would help us understand the information better. Glen Loates does the same thing when drawing a beaver lodge and dam in his book *Animal Babies*.

These and similar launchers create a desire to imitate these author/illustrators in situations where labeling would give the children's drawings, designs or models more meaning for the reader.

Letter writing

Through this routine children find many real uses for their letter-writing skills:

ANIMAl welfare INStitute
P.O. Box 3650
washington, DC 20007
V.S.A.

Dear sir or MaDame

Pleas sand me

A letter from a whale And a Whale Poster.
We are saveing whale's.

Yours true
Nicholas Baskwill
RR#1
Lawrencetown
Nova Scotia
BosIMo

Free Stuff for Kids is an excellent book, full of places to write to for posters and pamphlets and information about a variety of topics. *The Kids' World Almanac* by Margo McLoone-Basta and Alice Siegel provides names and addresses of museums, clubs, etc. that children might be interested in. For a "Dinosaur" theme I've used that book as a launcher, reading the section about museums with dinosaur exhibits. We drafted a letter and sent it, and within a few weeks had a delightful response enclosing pamphlets and information about dinosaurs.

This may seem very much like the language arts letter-writing routine, but I've found that during language arts we tend to look mostly at the author's use of letters as a story technique (for example, *The Jolly Postman*), and are thus inspired to write imaginary letters to characters or to favorite authors. A letter-writing launcher eliminates the need to create reasons for writing in the curriculum areas. The routine develops quite naturally: it's easy for children to make a connection to other people they know who have written away for things that have later arrived in the mail.

Lists

During language arts, this routine is used to look at the many different kinds of lists we find in real life or literature. We pay close attention to what lists look like and what kind of information they give, and we explore strategies for reading them.

In science, lists show up as items needed to conduct an experiment and as the names or types of plants or animals. In social studies, lists contain names of countries, cities, explorers, dates, etc. We notice that an index is an organized list of the contents of a book.

During a "Dinosaur" theme we received a fact sheet from the Tyrrell Museum in Alberta with a Paleo-phonics list of dinosaur names, their pronunciation and their meaning. We noticed right away that it was an alphabetic list, and that each scientific name was based on a particular characteristic of that dinosaur — either a physical attribute or the location where it was found. This way of presenting information was incorporated into the book we were writing on dinosaurs.

We used the routine also for other themes, particularly during a "Sea" theme when we were looking at organizing the names of various kinds of whales. In the end we decided to produce our own fact sheet of whale names and derivatives of those names.

Mapping

In language arts, the mapping routine gives children opportunities to practice the sequencing of events. In science, social studies and math, the exploration of a map can determine the scale of reproduction, calculate the distance between cities, chart the route an explorer took, etc.

A "Sea" theme lends itself to many mapping explorations. A good launcher for this routine is *The Children's Book of the Seas* by Jenny Tyler. It contains a map of the oceans, with interesting information about them, and stimulates the children to check what kinds of information other maps and globes might provide. Similarly, David Lambert's *A Field Guide to Dinosaurs* shows where the remains of particular dinosaurs have been found. The children won't settle for just an example or two from this book; they'll want to see each one!

Questioning

Questioning is a crucial skill for scientists, social scientists and mathematicians. Insight into what happens, how it happens, when it will happen again, and what would happen if something were changed depends on asking the right questions. Often children are asked to make a list of all the things they wonder about a topic, or of things they would like to know more about. A launcher helps prime the pump for putting that kind of thinking into words.

How Big Is a Brachiosaurus? by Susan Carroll lends itself to the further generation of questions and, perhaps, to an interest in discovering the answers. That book is also a good example of a different format for the organization of information, useful for the study of any topic. Using its design and structure as an example, children can develop class or individual books along the same lines.

Webbing

In language arts, webbing is a tool to help children organize their thoughts in a visual way. Most often webbing is used as a way to retell a familiar story or to outline a story the children intend to write.

In my classroom, webbing has also become became a very useful tool in science as a way to describe a series of events, as in the life cycle of a frog or a caterpillar. After reading about or observing the way a caterpillar changes from egg to caterpillar to butterfly to egg, some children chose to present their observations or understandings of the stages in a combination of drawings and labels:

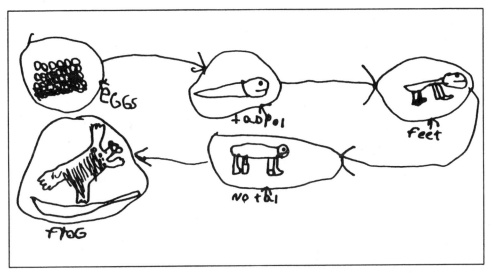

Robert Green's *Caterpillars* describes the life cycle of the Emperor Gum Moth and uses a web at the back of the book to summarize the process, thus providing a model for organizing information in such a manner. The children may decide to use the same method to record what happens during an experiment. The use of the launcher makes them aware of how an author uses the routine, then invites them to try it out for themselves when appropriate.

For younger children a timeline of events during a social studies theme becomes more meaningful when those events can be webbed in a combination of pictures and labels and seen to be part of a larger structure.

Mini-demonstrations

Mini-demonstrations are another useful type of routine: teacher-initiated discussions and/or actual demonstrations that help children focus on a particular strategy, problem or concept and explore possible solutions, alternative methodologies or means of organization. They help children to link what they already know or hypothesize to a new concept at hand. Although a mini-demonstration is usually followed by some activity related to it, that isn't always necessary.

Again using a "Sea" theme as an example, we can help the children make connections between the sea itself and the floating and sinking properties of objects by showing them how to brainstorm prior knowledge, then test an assortment of objects in pans of water and record their observations. In this way they not only discover the proerties of water, they also discover ways to share that information with others. More important, they learn that they can use writing as a thinking and planning tool.

Ads, brochures and pamphlets

This mini-demonstration focuses on the way information about a product or an item is presented. It provides children with real-life situations in which these formats are used and demonstrates how they are constructed.

I conducted such a demonstration during a "Home Sweet Home" theme. We had already discussed many aspects of the homes we live in — their construction, for instance — and the larger community our school is part of. Earlier, when we talked about writing a book about our area to send to other schools, I had thought that since we'd already written several group books during the year it might be time to invite the children, by means of a mini-demonstration, to try another format.

I first collected a variety of travel brochures about different historic sites and places of interest. During the demonstration I described the elements that make up such a brochure and showed the children the examples. They quickly noticed how colorful the pieces were, and that most of them included photographs. We paid close attention to the use of headings and the kinds of information those headings contained.

I raised the possibility that we might produce a brochure about the Parker's Cove area, and we broke into small groups to discuss what we might include. After about 10 minutes we came back together, pooled our ideas and made a list of some of the suggestions. This generated a lot of enthusiasm, but I didn't specifically invite the children to develop brochures of their own. However, when we came together the next day to think about the book we were going to write for other schools, Pam suggested we make a brochure instead. When we did so, other mini-demonstrations became necessary: how to select the most interesting material from too much information; how to write headings for each section; how to incorporate pictures and drawings, etc.

Parker's Cove School
Box 112 Granville Ferry
N.S. B0S 1K0

Parker's
Cove
School

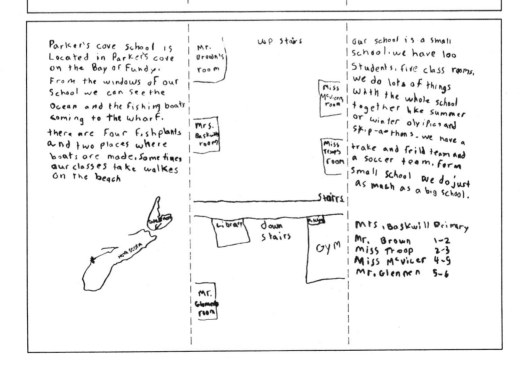

Parker's cove school is
located in Parker's cove
on the Bay of Fundy.
From the windows of our
school we can see the
ocean and the fishing boats
coming to the wharf.
there are four fishplants
and two places where
boats are made. sometimes
our classes take walkes
on the beach

up stairs

Mr.
Brown's
room

Miss
McVicar
room

Mrs.
Baskwill
room

Miss
Troop's
room

Stairs

Library   down
Stairs   School

                GYM

Mr.
Glennen
room

Our school is a small
school. we have 100
students. five class rooms.
we do lots of things
with the whole school
together like summer
or winter olyipics and
skip-a-thons. we have a
trake and freild team and
a soccer toam. form
small school we do just
as much as a big school.

Mrs. Baskwill Primary
Mr. Brown   1-2
Miss Troop   2-3
Miss McVicer   4-5
Mr. Glennen   5-6

Not all mini-demonstrations need to develop into something this elaborate. I could as easily have done the planning and organization myself, simply asking for input from the children. I could have prepared the pieces of text ahead of time, made ready a selection of headings and a choice of pictures. I could have talked about why I chose a particular heading and discarded another and how I decided what information to include. I could have laid out the brochure for them and left them with an invitation to try one of their own, giving them the option to follow up or not, now or later or never.

When time is available and ripe for this type of mini-demonstration, the children will modify and adapt what they've seen demonstrated so the project they undertake is something they own completely. As it turned out in this case, the children determined the direction we followed. Although I planned it initially, the project went off in a direction of its own.

Assembly-line activities

This routine demonstrates how to follow directions for such activities as a science experiment, a recipe, a craft or a trip. I try to choose an experiment related to the particular theme we're involved with at the time and enlarge the directions, using charts or an overhead projector, so the class can see the steps I'm following as I perform it.

For very young children, assembly-line activities should be as explicit as possible and utilize illustrations as well as bits of print. There are many sources of excellent experiments you might try. The book *The Scientific Kid* by Mary Stetten Carson contains 35 such activities presented in exactly this format. *Good Eats for Children* from the Ontario Milk Marketing Board has assembly-line cooking recipes ready to use.

During the theme "Take Flight" I demonstrated the making of a pinwheel, using the directions in the Carson book. I pointed out how I found the size of paper we would need, what the dotted lines meant, and how the X in the picture was explained in the print below it. I talked about reading the directions first to make sure I had all the materials I needed, and about following the directions step by step to get the pinwheels to turn out the way they were shown. I also mentioned how I went over the directions as if I were actually doing the activity, to make sure I understood how it went.

16

Following this mini-demonstration I had available five additional assembly-line activities, all related to the theme: bubbles, a wind sled, a boomerang, a helicopter, shadow puppets and two bird feeders. The children went in groups to the areas where I'd placed the direction cards and materials for their specific activities, and I circulated to give assistance or clarification if necessary.

Clipboard recording

Clipboard recording is on-the-spot recording of observations. As the name suggests, it uses a clipboard as the recording tool. The clipboard is placed beside an activity, a display or an ongoing experiment so the children can write their comments about what they notice, what they think has happened, or what they predict might happen next. For instance, during "float and sink" explorations the clipboard was hung near the water table. When the children finished testing various objects in the water they recorded their discoveries.

The clipboard can be placed near a terrarium or aquarium, or beside newly planted seeds. I've also placed one in the block area when the children have been constructing villages in preparation for mapping. Younger children record their ideas using a combination of pictures and words, often with functional spellings. All children record their names as well, in case others have questions they'd like to ask the observers.

We share these recordings briefly during the week and sometimes find conflicting reports. This sets up a beehive of activity as various children set out to reconfirm or change what was initially recorded. As time goes on, the children recognize the importance of recording things so others can read them. Their drawings become more detailed; they may use labels; they may even team up with someone else so they can get as much down as possible. The clipboard itself gives the children the feeling that they are really doing what scientists do. It has quite a grown-up feeling about it!

As in other mini-demonstrations, I record my own observations as well. I demonstrate to the class how I might use a combination of pictures and phrases to record what I notice. I also talk about why I chose to draw or write about that particular observation, and why I thought it was important at all. My demonstration helps the children get inside my head as a recorder and lets them in on some of the decisions I had to make when considering what to put down.

During our sharing sessions the children follow the same pattern to ask one another why they chose a particular item for their recording, or to request an explanation about something that may be unclear from the drawing.

Collections

All children enjoy collecting things. During a theme they can often be encouraged to collect particular items related to that theme. This mini-demonstration helps them see how a collection can be made more interesting, organized and available to someone else. Actually, I find I need more than one type of mini-demonstration when I'm thinking about collections, some dealing with organization and presentation and others with cataloging.

I usually begin by bringing in a collection of my own: buttons, rocks, shells, whatever I happen to be interested in at the time. I bring it in its "natural" state, not mounted or organized in any way. I talk about why I might want to organize it, who might be viewing it, where I might keep it, etc. I also have on hand an assortment of box lids, containers, colored paper, wallpaper, and cloth scraps for lining boxes. I let the children in on my thinking by talking about why I prefer one container over another, and why I choose which liner.

When the collection is attractively organized, I demonstrate ways to keep track of what I've collected so far, showing a notebook, file cards, scrapbook, etc. It's important to keep in mind that mini-demonstrations should be short, so I bring a collection that's easily manageable, one that can be organized in no more than about 10 minutes.

During a "Sea" theme I chose to do a mini-demonstration just after a beachcombing walk along the shore. Following the demonstration I suggested that the children take stock of what they had collected and plan how they might display it. The next day they brought in materials from home and set about organizing their collections with great enthusiasm.

Diaries

The diary routine is used quite effectively during language arts as the children record ongoing observations: the weather, for instance, or a series of events that happen over the course of a school week:

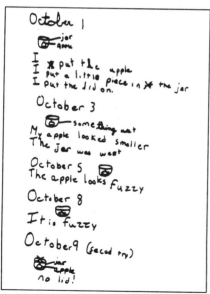

Usually I set this routine up through a series of mini-demonstrations, as the class and I work together to keep a diary of a particular event. I try to choose something that will happen rather quickly, with easy-to-observe changes — say within one or two weeks. Watching a seed sprout or a slice of apple dry is a good place to begin. I demonstrate the use of headings, the date, the time of day, the amount of information to include and useful drawings, as well as the actual observation of what changes have occurred.

After we've tried a diary together I invite the children to try one on their own, recounting developments that occur during daily classroom events. They may decide to work together or individually. Their observation skills, as well as their ability to determine what information is important, will improve over time.

This routine can also be used with launcher books such as *Caterpillar Diary* or *A Tadpole Diary*. These two Big Books are particularly useful when looking at different formats.

In-house museum

In my area it's seldom feasible to take the children to a museum, since the nearest is located far from the school and requires a lengthy bus trip. An in-house museum is an acceptable alternative that enables the school community to have firsthand experience with a museum and take part in the collection and presentation of information. It's a particularly good way to develop a collaborative spirit among the entire school body — and throughout the community if other schools or the public are invited to visit the display. Since this routine takes a lot of work and preparation, we usually undertake it only once during the course of the school year.

First, we invite a member of the provincial museum staff to come and speak to the whole school about the museum and what displays it has. That person usually brings along slides so the children can see what the museum actually looks like.

Back in their classrooms, each class brainstorms the displays we might include in our museum. Sometime during the week the school staff meets to decide what displays each group will be responsible for, based on the interests of its members.

Each class then sets to work on its contribution to the museum. The entire museum is assembled by an agreed-upon deadline and invitations are sent to other schools or to parents to attend. We organize small groups of children on a rotating basis to be in charge of the museum, to offer explanations or further information and to keep the displays tidy during the museum's open hours.

This is a highly effective way of getting the children involved in collecting, presenting and displaying information for others, as well as giving them firsthand experience with a museum and its functions.

Interviews

The question-and-answer routine mentioned in the *Whole Language Sourcebook* (p.32) describes one type of interview: questions to be asked are generated by the class prior to the interviewee's visit. As a mini-demonstration, the interview can also be a conversation between a guest and the teacher, where the teacher asks a set of prepared questions and takes notes of the answers.

I like to use these two routines in combination. First I use a mini-demonstration to show how to plan for an interview and carry it out. Then we use the question-and-answer routine to prepare for an interview of our own.

During a "Dinosaur" theme I interviewed the curator of one of our provincial museums about how displays are chosen and organized within the museum. I had previously explained to my guest the nature of this demonstration and alerted him that I might interrupt the interview from time to time to let the children in on why I was asking a particular question or what I was writing down in my notes. A demonstration interview is usually much shorter than one we all do together; I let it go on just long enough for the children to get a feeling for how it works.

The next day we broke into groups and brainstormed the questions we wanted to ask our next guest, a local geologist. Using these two routines in combination this way effectively helps children learn how to conduct an interview.

Naturalist's notebook

This is another type of diary routine, one that uses predominantly pictures or photographs to describe what is observed. Where the diary describes a series of changes observed over a period of time, the naturalist's notebook describes the variety of plants and animals observed at a particular location or given moment — it's more like a sketchbook, with detailed drawings but few words other than those used to label the plants or animals, if they're known, and to give the location and date.

I prefer to use this routine for outdoor studies. Not far from our school is Camp Hilles, a facility for day and overnight camps. Before taking a class to the camp I demonstrate the use of the naturalist's notebook by using an overhead or opaque projector to show samples of my notebook from other years. I talk about the media I've used (pencil, colored pencils, chalk, pastels, charcoal) and what the children might find to record when they get to the camp. I usually have material available for covers and an assortment of paper and fasteners for the children to make their own notebooks following the demonstration.

I build in a designated time during our stay at the camp (10-15 minutes three times a day) for observation and recording at various locations on the property: a sandy area, a grassy spot, a marsh, a woody slope, etc. I usually offer the children a variety of media to choose from, as well as magnifying glasses to take with them. Whenever possible I look for an opportunity to make and use these notebooks early in the school year; they are then saved and used throughout the year whenever we're involved in outdoor explorations.

Thinking journals

A thinking journal is a personal place for children to begin thinking on paper. It provides a place for young scientists and mathematicians to think about what they know and how they know it.

The journal itself is simply a notebook or scribbler, in our case kept in a central location within the classroom. Periodically I ask the children to think about a particular aspect of what we're doing in math, science or social studies and record their thinking in their journal. I try to have them use their journals at least every two or three weeks, not so often that it becomes monotonous or contrived, but often enough to provide some insight into their thinking at various stages of exploration.

I usually circulate and ask the children to read me their entries, making notes in my own book so I'll be sure to understand what the children intended to write — particularly important with beginning writers. Sometimes they write about what surprised them during an activity, or what they do when they get stuck figuring out their math, or what might have happened if such and such had changed.

I may use examples from the children's journals as demonstrations, or demonstrate how I write in my own. I don't worry about the complexity of the thinking the children record at this stage. It's just a beginning, providing the children with a starting place for using writing to reflect on what they're learning, or to think a problem through to solution. Eventually it becomes the natural thing to do.

Topic books

I first saw this routine used in the Freshfield Infant School in Formby, England. The teacher had loaded a large table with magazines and old calendars, and underneath it had placed a tray containing a large scrapbook for each child. Each scrapbook was also labeled with the title of a particular topic: cars, animals, people, cartoons, etc. Sometime during the day each child made his or her way to the table, located the appropriate scrapbook and set to work searching through the magazines for pictures related to the chosen topic, cutting them out and pasting them into the topic book.

To me, this seemed a good way for young children to learn some basic research skills: determining a topic, locating appropriate information (sometimes in the form of pictures), and deciding when the topic was complete. I decided to try using topic books, but to expand the routine beyond a simple gathering of pictures.

During a "Shelters" theme I conducted a mini-demonstration to set up the routine. First I talked about what a topic book is and why I might want to start one. Then I brainstormed possible topics I might choose. I decided on "Animal Shelters" and talked about the kinds of things I might include: pictures of birds' nests, birdhouses, wasps' nests, diagrams of ant hills, shells, trees, etc. I also talked about including something about the animal that lived in the shelter and writing that information below the appropriate picture or diagram. I had collected a few pictures in advance, so I put these into my scrapbook, along with a few sentences about them. I had an ample supply of scrapbooks available for any children who wanted to begin one of their own, and many did.

Children needn't begin their topic books immediately following your mini-demonstration. You might simply want to let them know that the materials are available and provide a flexible framework within which they can work on their own. This will help to prevent the undertaking of 25 topic books on animal shelters!

Another type of mini-demonstration that expands on the topic book idea is the "all about" book — *All About Dinosaurs,* for instance. For that the children and I pooled all of the information we had on the topic and worked together to develop it into a book.

This taking stock of what we know usually occurs at the end of a theme. It's a good way not only to recognize what it is we've learned through the course of the theme, but also to develop something that can later be used by other children in the school; sometimes we even donate the books to the library or Bookmobile to be shared in other parts of our county. As we work through the process of producing this particular type of book, we learn a lot about how non-fiction books are structured, their various components, and the informational style of writing.

Summary

Whatever curriculum area you're focusing on — science, social studies or math — there are many routines that can help children make use of the knowledge they already have, employ their natural propensity for asking questions, and provide opportunities for them to refine and expand their knowledge as they share it with others. I've described some that work well for me, but as you examine your own classroom situation, and the things you're already doing, other possibilities will come to mind.

An interrelated use of themes provides a framework for children that makes it easier for them to use their vast capabilities and growing understandings. As they explore various aspects of a theme, they constantly make connections. Instead of having to cope with a day artificially divided into small, isolated segments, they have those segments tied together for them into a sensible whole. A theme provides common experiences for the learning community and allows the children to share their language discoveries and curricular links.

An interrelated curriculum, woven around a broad thematic base, allows children to do what they naturally do best: make connections in order to make sense out of their learning environment.

Note

There are many excellent trade titles available, and more appearing all the time. You should make good use of book clubs and book fairs as well as book stores and libraries. Listed below are a few other sources I've found useful, to add to your own:

Books for Young Explorers Series and World Explorers Series
    National Geographic Society
    17 and M Streets NW
    Washington DC 20036

Bookshelf
    Scholastic (see addresses page ii)

Cricket Magazine
    Box 2670
    Boulder, CO 80322

David Suzuki Series
    Stoddart Publishing Co. Limited
    34 Lesmill Road
    Toronto, ON M3B 2T6

Elementary Science Study Series
    McGraw Hill School Division
    Box 25308
    Oklahoma City, OK 73125

Examining Your Environment Series
    Holt Rinehart and Winston of Canada Ltd.
    55 Horner Avenue
    Toronto, ON M8Z 4X6

Glen Loates North American Wildlife Series
    Crabtree Publishing Co. Limited
    120 Carlton Street # 309
    Toronto, ON M5A 4K2

Ontario Science Centre Books
    Kids Can Press
    585½ Bloor Stree W
    Toronto, ON M6G 1K5

OWL Publications
    51 Front Street East
    Toronto, ON M5E 1B3

National Wildlife Federation Publications
    1412 16th Street NW
    Washington DC 20036

Vancouver Environmental Project
    University of British Columbia Press
    Vancouver, BC V6T 1W5

Titles in the New Directions series

Each book in the New Directions series deals with a single, practical classroom topic or concern, teaching strategy or approach. Many teachers have recognized the collegial and encouraging tone in them — not surprising, since most of them have been written by practicing teachers. Indeed, if you have an idea for a New Directions title of your own, we encourage you to contact the Publishing Division, Scholastic Canada.

Existing titles include:

In Canada, order from: Scholastic-TAB Publications Ltd., 123 Newkirk Road, Richmond Hill, ON L4C 3G5

In the United States, order from: Scholastic Inc., Box 7502, Jefferson City, MO 65102